SOUL FOOD – There's Hope!

By Linda Pearl Ramnath

SOUL FOOD – There's Hope!

Contents

i. Introduction

1. Why do we fear?

2. The red-back spider

3. Stagnant water

4. Food for thought!

5. Live life loud!

6. Matters of the heart

7. Rejoice, see who comes ...

8. Full of hot air

9. Times, they are changing

10. Anger is like murder

11. See the empty tomb!

12. Get up and keep moving!

13. Attention, what is your Intention?

14. The new command!

15. Marriage is like two peas in a pod!

16. Trust

17. One or the other...

18. When broken is needed

19. A Star is born

20. Other Works

Introduction

SOUL FOOD – There's Hope! is the fifth booklet in the series of SOUL FOOD. In these times of great distress, we all need to search for something positive. We need a source of hope to sustain us in order to confidently face each new day. Hope is forward looking and propels us on, even when there appears to be nothing to look forward to. Interestingly, it is only when we connect with other people that we realise that our problems are much smaller than we make them out to be.

In this booklet, SOUL FOOD – There's Hope! the reader gets comforting words of life from the Word of God. You are able to tap into a source that will help you transcend the earthly worries and give you wings like an eagle so that your spirit can soar high. When our spirits are healed, healing also comes to our mind and body. Read SOUL FOOD – There's Hope! and be empowered to live an overcoming life.

Why do we fear?

By day and by night, we have protection. The Lord led His people towards the promised land under Moses' leadership. He had a supernatural layer of protection over them (Exodus 13:21).

In our lives, not all things go smoothly. There are seasons where we sail on a calm sea and everything goes according to plan. Then there are seasons when we get struck down by lightning bolts, one after the other. It shakes us and turns our world upside down. We scramble to our feet eventually and try to pick up the pieces after the storm in our life has abated. We look like drenched chickens after a heavy downpour. Yet, something deep within us says we must go on.

When a bad season comes along, it is a season and not a once only event. Soon after we think we have sufficiently recovered from one ordeal; another one comes along. Like a sail boat, the wind is taken out of our ship and we find ourselves at the mercy of the elements. We cling onto whatever shreds we can find, hoping we will survive. Something deep within us says, 'I've got to hold on'.

The amazing thing about the human spirit is its resilience factor. Against all odds, we hold on to that tiny glimmer of hope. Why is that so? Whether we realize it or not, we are all created in the image of God (Genesis 1:27). This means we are wired with a God factor in our DNA. Our souls reach out to God. We acknowledge that there is something bigger than ourselves. We have hope that miraculously we will get through even the darkest days of our soul.

When I read how God supernaturally led the Israelites out of slavery in Egypt and met their every need out in the wilderness, I was awestruck. They not only had protection but they could go on with their journey by day AND by night. In day seasons, when we can see clearly, God leads us under His umbrella of protection. In night seasons, when our world is too dark, we are able to still go on because the Lord has a pillar of fire, burning steadily above us. We look up to His supernatural provision and we are enabled to chart our course in those night seasons.

Why do we fear? Why are we anxious? Why do we think we are never going to make it through the night? As sure as there is day and night, there is hope for every one of us.

Seasons come and go and bad things happen to even good people, but God is constant. He is our source of life, He is our source of strength, He is our source hope and our protection. We just need to put our life into His divine hand and allow Him to lead us by day and by night. Matthew 28:20b (BSB) tells us," And surely I am with you always, to the very end of the age." ◊

The red-back spider

Beware of the red-back spider! It sits there very quietly and carefully ponders its move. Its intention is clear; there can be no error of judgement! It has to be precise in its deadly execution; absolutely no room for error! Beware of the person who, in the guise of friendship, wants to suck the life blood out of you. They start off with lots of sweetness and concern for you. They offer you a listening ear and lots of comfort. You think how blessed you are to have them come into your life. When you have warmed up sufficiently to them, they start to sink their tentacles into you. Deeper and deeper those tentacles go, without you even realizing it. It is like deadly sugar-coated pills. You think its candy yet you do not realise there is lethal stuff in it, designed to slowly suck the life blood out of you.

Slowly it dawns on you that their friendship is pretty full on and their interactions are becoming too much for you to cope with. You try to reason it out but because the toxin is already in your system, you cannot make out fact from fiction. The deadly red-back spider has just got itself another prey!

What do you do? Take it to the Lord in prayer. This is a battle that only He can fight and win. Remember, the weapons of our warfare are not carnal but mighty to the pulling down of strongholds – 2 Corinthians 10:4. Strongholds need someone mighty to pull them out and destroy their works. ◊

Stagnant water

When you are stuck in one place, the life flow of living water is stopped. You become like stagnant water, which is stuck and going nowhere. A puddle of water can soon become dried up by the sun or it can become murky and attract organisms that contaminate it, making it of no use for anything.

People can become stagnant in life, where the life flow is blocked for some reason. Their spirits get crushed and they become 'dry bones'. The light in their eyes start to fade and their zeal for life starts to dwindle. Very often illness takes hold of their bodies and they use it as a crutch to hobble about. This illness is often rooted in psychological issues.

Unresolved conflict is like cancer to the soul. It is often an unwarranted burden on the recipient and those connected to that individual. The consequence is similar to stagnant water; trapped and foul smelling. Instead of being a source of life and enrichment like flowing water, those who are like stagnant water, invariably become a burden to others. Proverb 18:14 talks about this - The spirit of a man can endure his sickness, but who can survive a broken spirit?

What can one do to liberate the soul trapped in unresolved conflict? Conflict resolution offers various possible solutions, which involve proactive measures. Moving out from stagnant water to living water is a deliberate choice. The mind is a very powerful thing and has power to destroy or liberate a person. God has provided us with the solution - Proverbs 17:22 says, "A joyful heart is good medicine, but a broken spirit dries up the bones." There is hope; Psalm 34:18-20 tells us that the LORD is near to the brokenhearted and saves those who are crushed in spirit. Take control of your life, steer your destiny towards the flow. Be a spring brook, not a stagnant pool. ◊

Food for thought!

Ponder on these things…! The identity we have is … that thing which defines us. We shape our lives by the decisions we make but are influenced by things around us. We possess the ability to make choices that fashion and form the path we take on life's journey.

In the Bible we read of numerous characters who led either triumphant lives or defeated lives. How do we know which is the right path for us? True, if you are born into a family and are part of a specific culture, there are unwritten rules and obligations that regulate your actions. Right from the onset of time, we know that God gave the first man freedom of choice. Inadvertently, the choices we make determines the life we live!

Throughout history so many wars have been fought; most of them were religious ones. When you see religion as a man-made construct, you see the covert agenda; to suppress and dominate. The priests and scribes were so obsessed with religious practices that it was the end all and be all. Even in the Lord Jesus's time, the Pharisees and Sadducees diametrically opposed Him, based on religious sanctification rituals. Their religiosity blinded them to the reality of His message of love and reconciliation.

Christ Jesus came to restore relationship with man and God (John 12:46). By following the example of how Jesus lived, we can live a life that is in right relationship with God. When He ascended to heaven, Jesus promised the Holy Spirit to lead and guide us into living righteous lives (John 15:26). We may not be able to control all factors in our lives, like our birth and cultural identity, but we can tap into the source greater than ourselves to lead and guide us into living a productive and pleasing life.

History informs us of the past and gives us lessons for the future. When we look at

Biblical characters, we see themes of pride and humbleness recurring. Samson was a mighty warrior who defeated his enemies singlehandedly, but conceit and disobedience led to his demise. The same was true of King Saul and many kings who were arrogant and filled with pride.

Oftentimes, people who put the welfare of others before themselves like Queen Esther and Ruth, were rewarded beyond their expectations. Interestingly, of the 40 kings who ruled in Old Testament times, only eight were good. They were obedient to God and did what was right and pleasing in His sight. As a result, their kingdom prospered and their people lived in peace.

When we give allegiance to God as the starting point of our lives, we have right standing relationships with others. Our lives become fruitful and blessed. This is a simple truth, tested by time. Yet, many people do not grasp it. They think they are the captain of their own ship, forgetting who it is that gives wind to their sails. Is this not the height of pride and self-centredness? What type of life are you living – self-centred or God-centred? ◊

Live life loud!

The often-used cliche - 'Live life loud!' is generally used to represent boisterous living. However, in a wider context, musical images of loudness relate to a trumpet or bugle call that get people's attention. A clanging bell on the other hand, is a bothersome sound. Visual images also carry meaningful messages; a giant sunflower reaches majestically towards the heavens, whereas weeds annoy us and grow where they are not welcome.

If you had a bird's eye view of your life, how would it look - sunflower or weed; trumpet or clanging bell? 1 Corinthians 13:1 talks about a resounding gong and clanging cymbal in relation to people who are obnoxious because they do not have love towards their fellow men. They are people you want to run far away from.

Aren't we here to be a blessing? We read in Isaiah 52:7 (NKJV), "How beautiful upon the mountains Are the feet of him who brings good news, Who proclaims peace, Who brings glad tidings of good things, Who proclaims salvation, Who says to Zion, 'Your God reigns!'"

Some people do not realise that we all have an expiry date. They are so obsessed with accumulating things that they forget to live life. They aggressively work for their things, rather than for enjoying life and in the process, the things shape who they are. Psalm 103:15 (NKJV) says, "As for man, his days are like grass; As a flower of the field, so he flourishes." When you are gone, would people remember you as a noxious weed or a bold sunflower?

Let's make our sojourn here a remarkable one. Live life loud in a way that attracts rather than repels people. We can do this if we have a signpost. Isaiah 40:7-8 (NKJV) says, "The grass withers, the flower fades, Because the breath of the LORD blows upon it; Surely the people are grass. The grass withers, the flower fades, But the word of our God stands forever." When we live our life according to God's word, we have a solid foundation. We can then live a life of significance and worth. ◊

Matters of the heart

Matters of the heart require deep thought to respond to instead of hasty reaction. After seeking prayerfully, situations that appear complex, we go to the source for answers. We know that the best counsel comes from God's Holy Spirit, who leads and guides us towards the best outcome.

Two words come to mind; honour and respect. When you honour someone, you place them in a position of authority and you reverence that authority. You dare not talk carelessly or harshly in their presence. You dare not raise your voice or utter profane words either. You show the utmost respect and display graceful behaviour. Why? It is because their position commands such respect and responsibility.

Unless you are intoxicated or not in your right state of mind, you know better to challenge a police officer or judge. Why? They have earned the title of authority and respect. The Bible tells us in the Ten Commandments that children are to honour their parents. There are no supporting clauses for what parents ought to do for gaining that respect, but there is a direct conditional clause for children. When children obey the command to honour their parents, they are given a guarantee that life will go well with them (Deuteronomy 5:16).

This means that they will prosper in what they do, they will be blessed and they will live peaceably with others.

If we unpack the word 'honour', we find it relates to other key action words. Honour is synonymous with obedience, respect and caring for the welfare of that person in authority, whom we esteem highly. Attached to this honour is a high level of moral worth. You honour someone who is morally upright. The common reference is 'the man is worth his salt'. Morally upright people are said to be worth their salt and are good role models.

When you display respect towards your parents, you put their needs above yours. Respect cannot be bought; it has to be earned. Think of ways in which you can show respect for your parents. They say a good parent is one who has unconditional love for their child. This love in its purist form is the love that God, our Heavenly Father displays to us. While we were yet sinners, He sent His Son, Jesus to die for our sins so that we could be pardoned and be in right standing with Him. That is our Heavenly Father's part; our part is to make right by acknowledging the wrong doing, repenting of it and changing direction. In so doing, we will be in right standing with God, who loves the sinner but hates the sin.

Why do we have so many issues of the heart, especially when they relate to the ones we love? Disobedience, sin and selfishness are trace elements that make for a bad soil in one's heart. Very often the root of these negative elements is tied up to material things.

When our focus is on things rather than on relationships, there is a hefty price to pay. We can never get enough out of things; we want more and more. It is an insatiable goblin that soon becomes master and we become its docile slaves. It's a trap that many people fall into and from which there is no reprieve. That is why the Lord Jesus said that it is easier for a camel to go through the eye of a needle than a rich man to enter the kingdom of God (Matthew 19:24).

What do we do when we find we are between a rock and a hard place? We go to a place where we can transcend the boundaries that our situation dictates to us. Isaiah 40:31 (NKJV) says, "But those who wait on the LORD Shall renew their strength; They shall mount up with wings like eagles,

They shall run and not be weary, They shall walk and not faint."

Matters of the heart can weigh you down heavily. Do not try to work things out on your own when you can transcend, get direction and help so that you too can soar like the eagle - powerful and majestic. ◊

Rejoice, see who comes ...

What is Christmas all about? It's about joy! We rejoice because the Lord has come! The lyrics of the famous Christmas carol read: "Joy to the world, the Lord is come. Let earth receive her King! Let every heart prepare Him room. And heaven and nature sing..." We jump for joy because the King has come!

The lyrics continues with the next proclamation, "He rules the world with truth and grace and makes the nations prove the light of His righteousness and wonders of His love..." Where is the evidence? Jeremiah 23:6 calls Him the Lord our righteousness. Zachariah 9:9 and Matthew 21:5-7 says, "Behold your King comes to you... He is just and having salvation." Isaiah 9:6-7 says, "For unto us a child is born... He will reign ... with justice and righteousness..."

Is Christmas just a celebration for Christians who commemorate the birth of Jesus Christ? It is for followers of Christ, who look up to Him as their King and Saviour. As King, Jesus Christ rules and as Savour He saves. If Jesus is King and Saviour in your life, then He rules and saves. This implies that we should be radiant in appearance rather than disillusioned and downtrodden. How many faces have you seen that reflect they are carrying the weight of the world on their shoulders?

If you desire to be in relationship with the Lord Jesus Christ and follow Him closely, you cannot be downcast and disillusioned. Following Him means turning away and moving in the direction that His Spirit is leading you. Trying to do things in your own strength to fix situations instead of entrusting it to the King and Saviour, is foolishness.

Who has the King of Glory come for? Isaiah 57:15 tells us He has come for the oppressed and humble of spirit, to restore the spirit of the lowly and revive the heart of the contrite. This King of Glory who is mighty in power is the creator and ruler of the universe. Isaiah 43:11 says, "I, yes I am the

LORD, and there is no Savior but Me." We should rejoice because our King has come. Psalm 118:24 says we should rejoice and be glad.

Those who look to the Lord Jesus Christ are radiant. Read Psalm 34 and rejoice. The King has come to save you and give you peace and eternal life - read John 10:10. ◊

Full of hot air

The expression, 'He is just hot air', denotes emptiness. It relates to something that carries no value. Sometimes you might get a parcel delivered to you in a big box. When you open it up, you realise it is just a small item, which is surrounded by air pillows. I received some vitamins which arrived at my door in a box twice as big as a shoe box. So much waste of space!

In a culture where reading a soft copy of a book has been replaced by online copies or eBooks, and even audio books, the enjoyment of turning a page and reflecting, seems to be lost. People consume rather than digest; they grow in knowledge but do not ponder over the deep truths. Their knowledge base becomes wider but their depth of understanding becomes more shallow. Knowledge without wisdom is folly! Those who speak without 'thinking' are considered unwise or foolish.

Gaining wisdom involves reflection, time to ponder, to think deeply, absorb and digest knowledge. In a world that is so hurried and almost everything is instant, how many of us do retreat to a quiet space? We are bombarded with blaring television screens, electronic billboards and hand-held devices that literally demand our attention. We see a lot, we hear a lot and we talk a lot! All too often people talk a lot of hot air.

We are living in a phenomenal age, a sizeable advancer in all areas of life - on earth and in outer space. The gaining of knowledge has reached unprecedented levels. Yet, how rich are we in the acquiring of understanding and wisdom?

Daniel 12:4 and Revelation 22:10 predictions resonate very loudly to our present times. Daniel 12:4 (BSB) says, "But you, Daniel, shut up these words and seal the book until the time of the end. Many will roam to and fro, and knowledge will increase." Revelation 22:10 (BSB) says, "Then he told me, 'Do not seal up the words of prophecy in this book, because the time is near.'" Daniel 10:14 says, "Now I have come to explain to you what will happen to your people in the latter days, for the vision concerns those days." Look around you, are we not living in such end times?

2 Timothy 3:1-8 talk about the last days. Verses 2-4 (BSB) say, "For men will be lovers of themselves, lovers of money, boastful, arrogant, abusive, disobedient to their parents, ungrateful, unholy, unloving, unforgiving, slanderous, without self-control, brutal, without love of good, traitorous, reckless, conceited, lovers of pleasure rather than lovers of God."

As the new year dawns, what are your yearnings? Is it just hot air promises and relentless hot air speeches or are you going to stand resolute as a person of action who is worth his salt? ◊

Times, they are changing

Times are changing at an overwhelming rate. Are they for the better or for the worst? Paging through a Centenary Celebration book, revealed marvelous insights into the country I now call home. From working the earth amidst much toil and camaraderie, man has devised mechanical implements to make life easier and better. Now, we find ourselves in an advanced technological and digital age where computers can outsmart the average human being. These superseding pursuits ought to propel us to a bigger, better world. Indeed, we seemed to have outsmarted ourselves! Children know more than parents and babies are astoundingly techno savvy.

We know that there is a cost to everything. Ponder on this: is humanity really advancing. No doubt, great advances confront us in every sphere of life. The Beatles penned a song with lyrics that read, "look at all those lonely people..." That was just a few decades ago and times were hard. Now, we seem to be living in the lap of luxury but the social and emotional barometers of men and women are nearing reserve tank. Why is that so? Where is the cohesiveness? Where is the camaraderie? Why is mental health the number one item on the world agenda? Where is our source of strength, life and liberty? Where is that peace and unspeakable joy?

If you want the purest water, you gravitate to the source. Every mountain climber knows that the higher you get, the better the water tastes. Matthew 11:28 says, "Come to me, all you who are weary and burdened, and I will give you rest." Psalm 34:8 says, "Taste and see that the LORD is good; blessed is the one who takes refuge in him." How do we get there? Proverbs 3:5 talks about trusting in the Lord with all your heart and not leaning on your own understanding.

The evidence of that solid foundation is found in Isaiah 26:4 that says, "Trust in the LORD forever, for the LORD, the LORD himself, is the Rock eternal." If you march forward towards the source of life, liberty and freedom, you will find that fullness of life and unspeakable joy. ◊

Anger is like murder

Anger is a powerful and potent human emotion. It has potential to annihilate almost anything. Anger stems from discord and if not dealt with, it can sprout and develop into a bitter root that anchors itself deep within the human heart.

When anger takes root in someone's life, it inadvertently divides the spirit and the soul. No wonder, words of wisdom echo, 'Don't let the sun go down on your wrath'. Anger can fester and multiply at an alarming rate, like cancerous cells in the body. You have to seek out an antidote if you want to survive. Like cancer, if left untreated, anger will be the death of you.

Anger is treated very seriously in the Bible. It is equivalent to murder. Matthew 5:21-25 has a strong teaching about anger. It opens with these words: 'You have heard that our ancestors were told, 'You must not murder. If you commit murder, you are subject to judgment.' Read the full context.

Anger not resolved is more costly than you realise. Not only can your unsolved issues incur significant costs via lawsuits, the personal costs are even more detrimental to your soul. 1 John 3:15 says, "Anyone who hates a brother or sister is a murderer, and you know that no murderer has eternal life residing in him."

What does it matter if you have significant wealth, yet you have driven away the ones who love you? Who can share your happiness when you have detached yourself from your loved ones, all because you cannot deal with your anger? Who will be there to stand with you in good times and bad times? Friends are there for a season and certainly fair-weather friends are only there when the weather (life situation) is good.

Most importantly, anger that is not addressed, kills. The person who you think has offended you becomes dead to you. You have killed them in your heart and mind. To you they are dead: they do not exist. You go on living, knowing they are dead to you, yet they could be very much in your presence on a day-to-day basis. You think you have killed them and they have no part in your life. On the contrary, it is you who is dying. You are living a lie and pretending that all is well. You soul is not at peace and you know it.

The solution is surprisingly simple; it is wrapped up in forgiveness. Jesus Christ was murdered. He did no wrong but even He pleaded to God the Father to forgive the ones who killed Him. He knew what judgement awaits those who murder. He interceded on their behalf. Likewise, when we sincerely ask God to forgive us our sins, like a torrential rain falling on a dirty car, He washes us clean. He washes us, restores us, renews us and fills us with newness of life. Old things are passed away as He does a new work in our lives. We become a new creature in Christ Jesus and are able to walk in the fullness of life, no longer chained to the old. We know that the wages of sin is death but the gift of God is eternal life through Jesus Christ. ◊

See the empty tomb!

Death is defeated,
Mourning to rejoicing.
Once condemned,
Now conqueror.

Behold, He comes,
Lowly baby no more.
Majestic King of kings,
Lord of lords.

Your response?
Condemned or accepted?
Penalty or privilege?
Eternal life or death?

Adam had a choice,
Pontius Pilot had a choice.
Judas Iscariot had a choice,
You have a choice!

One moment in time,
The price for all was paid.
Death, where is your sting?
Grave, where is your victory?

What's it going to be?
Lucifer was chief musician,
Pride goes before a fall.
Cain devised evil against his brother, Abel.

We are *all* marked.
Are you marked with the cross?
Are you destined for eternal damnation?
We all have a choice.

Choose wisely this day,
Your whole life depends on it!
You were bought with a price.
Life for life - a finished work on the cross.

John 3:16-18,
Your love letter.
Open it!
Freedom! ◊

Get up and keep moving!

So, you have been dealt a major setback! You can't seem to move on. All you do is lie there and burrow in the situation that seems so insurmountable. You wish you could just curl up and die. Well, *don't!* As long as you have breath, you have life!

If you cannot even crawl, the fact that you inch your way forward, is admirable. You have to move forward. Don't look back as this will hinder your progress.

You say, 'This is so hard'. I fully agree. But when you look ahead to the prize that awaits you, it will give you the strength to keep moving on - see 2 Timothy 4:8.

Don't listen to the lies of the enemy of your soul. He is the accuser of the brethren since the beginning of time - read Genesis 3:1-4; 2 Corinthians 2:11 and Revelation 12:10. Know that he is a defeated foe, trying to intimidate and trick you by using logic.

Remember facts speak for themselves and the truth will always set you free - John 8:31-32.

We *can* find refuge for our souls in the midst of the turmoil. Matthew 11:28 (NLT) says, "Then Jesus said, "Come to me, all of you who are weary and carry heavy burdens, and I will give you rest." Remember, now is not the time to quit. Get up and keep moving. ◊

Attention, what is your Intention?

With the current situation that has caught the attention of the entire world, the pivotal question is; what is *your* intention? The world has been brought to its knees. Never before in our known history has such a cataclysmic event crippled mankind like this. Bustling streets teaming with millions of people suddenly appear surreal, like ghost town scenes from a horror movie. Elsewhere, no more pushing and shoving hordes of people into an already crowded train. Tropical paradise of the rich and famous, now gape into vast empty rooms, collecting dust. It took one virus, deadly and unseen, to bring a drop- dead moment in history. What do you do? What do you think? Where do you go? Now what?

Social isolation, social distancing, social networking, social media. Social everything yet no socialising, no human contact, no touch, no pat, no hugs, no kisses, no handshake, nothing! If we view ourselves as social beings, why have we been driven so far apart from each other in recent years? Texting on the dinner table, texting while traveling, walking and even driving. See the invisible walls we have created between the ones closest to us. So called 'online friends' – do 'they' really care about our down times? It is a social parade for the most 'likes' – such insatiable appetites for 'what'?

When self is paraded on the 'catwalk', reality takes a backstage. The image supersedes the real person. Keeping up appearances becomes all-consuming till it consumes the person. Self-glorifying is self- defying and self-destructive. Pride goes before a fall – see Proverbs 16:18. Ask that age-old Lucifer! True love loves with lumps, bumps and all. It does not cover up with a thick paste or don fake additions to distort the real you. What you see is what you get when people are not afraid to be themselves.

This global pandemic has certainly got the brains well oiled; young and old alike. Existential questions have people looking hard and fast into their soul. In Job 11:7-9 (NIV) we read: "Can you fathom the mysteries of God? Can you probe the limits of the Almighty? They are higher than the heavens above- what can you do? They are deeper than the depths below-what can you know? Their measure is longer than the earth and wider than the sea."

The Genesis account of the creation of man in Genesis 1:26-28, is a far cry from what man has become. Seeds of jealousy and envy germinate into weeds of hatred, anger, greed, lust, violence, murder and similar destructive vices. Oh, how vile has the human heart become!

Theories and conspiracies aside, at the end you stand alone! One life, one individual, one soul – what is your intention? In the midst of all the contention, the still small voice of your soul navigates you to your Maker – see 1 Corinthians 2:11. Nothing is hid from Him, no one escapes Him, past present and future sit smugly in the palm of His hand. Do we dare to question Almighty God? Read Job 39-42 for yourself. Sooner or later, we will meet our Maker! You stand alone and He awaits your reply. The day of reckoning is fast approaching. ◊

The new command!

Unity is synonymous with being in one mind; being in accord, in agreement and being together on something. When we are agreeable on something, conflict is not present. A happy, cordial relationship is fostered and maintained. This directly impacts the mind and the body, sending positive vibes which penetrate and recharge the atmosphere.

Why is it that you can tell from a distance when a new couple are on a date? Their body signals speak louder than their words. They are often blissfully unaware of those around them and they certainly don't spend the time telling each other their problems. Have you watched an elderly couple walk on the beach or sit in a park? They too are at peace with themselves as they take in the scene and enjoy the moment.

Why is it that people talk so much, yet fail to listen to what they are actually saying? Is it that they love their voice or perhaps love an audience or maybe perhaps so many things vie for their attention that they can't filter properly what is significant?

When we truly love someone or something, we invest valuable time and resources into it. We do not take it for granted and neither do we make hasty or foolish decisions. Investing is key to building something that will last a long time. We invest in relationships that we value and we expect a good return on it.

They say the most important resource we have is 'time'. So, ask yourself, 'Do I use my time wisely?' Any aging parent would trade an expensive gift for 'time' with their loved ones. If your whole life flashed before your eyes in a micro-minute, what would be the single thing that stood out?

The Lord Jesus gave two key commands, which hinge onto each other. Firstly, love the Lord your God with all your heart, and secondly, love your neighbour (fellow man) as yourself - Matthew 22:38 and Luke 10:27. Imagine what this world would be like if people lived by those commands! When we have our focus in the right place; honouring God and respecting our fellow man, we will be outward focused rather than inward focused. We would put the welfare of others before our own. We would love and respect others and not be consumed with self-gratification.

We would walk in love and unity and develop, strong, healthy relationships. Did you know that happy people are healthier people? They recharge the atmosphere and positively impact those around them. The recipe is simple: honour God and respect others. Colossians 3:14-15 (NIV) says, "And over all these virtues put on love, which binds them all together in perfect unity. Let the peace of Christ rule in your hearts, since as members of one body you were called to peace." Just a simple word - 'unity', possesses atomic proportions of energy to supernaturally transform our lives. This enables us to live in peace and unity. What a world that would be! ◊

Marriage is like two peas in a pod!

One of the most problematic relationships of all mankind is the marriage relationship. It has caused untold grief to men, women and children alike. It has fragmented society and is the scourge of humanity. This was not the original plan of God. We were meant to live in love and unity and have a blessed union. By abiding by God's word, we can smoothly circumnavigate through our marriages. Here are 7 scripture references from ESV Bible.

Togetherness equals companionship
Ecclesiastes 4:9-12 says, "Two are better than one, because they have a good reward for their toil. For if they fall, one will lift up his fellow. But woe to him who is alone when he falls and has not another to lift him up! Again, if two lie together, they keep

warm, but how can one keep warm alone? And though a man might prevail against one who is alone, two will withstand him—a threefold cord is not quickly broken." When we have God in the centre of our marriage, it is like a threefold cord that cannot be easily broken.

Agreement
Matthew 18:19 say, "Again I say to you, if two of you agree on earth about anything they ask, it will be done for them by my Father in heaven." Being on one-page equals having the same agenda. Agreement implies unity and where there is unity, God commands a blessing.

Action and consequences
Ephesians 5:22-24 says, "Wives, submit to your own husbands, as to the Lord. For the husband is the head of the wife even as Christ is the head of the church, his body, and is himself its Saviour. Now as the church submits to Christ, so also wives should submit in everything to their husbands." Submit means acquiesce, concur and agree. This is to synchronize and walk together in harmony.
Ephesians 5:25-26 says, "Husbands, love your wives, as Christ loved the church and gave himself up for her, that he might

sanctify her, having cleansed her by the washing of water with the word." Love implies showing affection, tenderness and friendship. Your wife should be your best friend. You both are a complement to each other, not competition. 1 Peter 3:7 says, "Likewise, husbands, live with your wives in an understanding way, showing honour to the woman as the weaker vessel, since they are heirs with you of the grace of life, so that your prayers may not be hindered." By showing understanding, you are being considerate, supportive and appreciative of your wife. She doesn't want a million dollars, instead she wants you!

Love conquers all
1 Corinthians 13 is commonly known as the love chapter. There are great gems contained in the 13 verses. 1 Corinthians 13:4-7 says, "Love is patient and kind; love does not envy or boast; it is not arrogant or rude. It does not insist on its own way; it is not irritable or resentful; it does not rejoice at wrongdoing, but rejoices with the truth. Love bears all things, believes all things, hopes all things, endures all things." There are 15 gems in these 55 words. Imagine one person wearing 15 jewels – how radiant they would look!

The importance of the armour of God
Ephesians 6:12-13 says, "For we do not wrestle against flesh and blood, but against the rulers, against the authorities, against the cosmic powers over this present darkness, against the spiritual forces of evil in the heavenly places. Therefore, take up the whole armour of God, that you may be able to withstand in the evil day, and having done all, to stand firm." Like every country has security forces to protect its citizens, every marriage needs an angelic army to safeguard its frontiers. ◊

Trust

There is a song that says, 'Count your blessings, name them one by one ... and it will surprise you what the Lord has done! In this period of uncertainty and great fear that the world has never tasted before, we need an anchor to rest our souls. We cannot trust the hype that media creates, neither can we put our confidence in men in authority, who themselves are standing on shaking ground. But we can and must look up to the Creator of the heavens and earth who holds all things in His mighty hand.

The human heart can grow very faint in the midst of turmoil. We need something bigger than ourselves to carry us through. The wisest man, King Solomon said in Proverbs 3:5-6 (NIV), "Trust in the Lord with all your heart and lean not on your own understanding; in all your ways submit to him and he will make your paths straight."

We *can* put our trust in the One who is able to save us. Psalm 23:4 (ESV) says, "Even though I walk through the valley of the shadow of death, I will fear no evil, for you are with me; your rod and your staff, they comfort me." Again, Psalm 138:7 (NIV) says, "Though I walk in the midst of trouble, you preserve my life. You stretch out your hand against the anger of my foes; with your right hand you save me."

When our hope and trust is fixed on our Savour, our hearts do rest. Use this T.R.U.S.T. acronym when you see that storm coming:

Take your troubles to the only One who is *Truthful*.
Reach out to the *Rock* of your soul.
Understand the *Unending* Love Father God has for you.
Seek His *Security* and *Strength* to cover you.
Talk to the lover of your soul who holds *Time* in His hands.

What a blessed assurance we have that we can ride out the storm. The song concludes with this verse: 'So amid the conflict, whether great or small, Do not be discouraged; God is over all. Count your many blessings; angels will attend, Help and comfort give you to your journey's end.' Be blessed! ◊

One or the other...

Here is food for thought: "No one can serve two masters. Either you will hate the one and love the other, or you will be devoted to the one and despise the other. You cannot serve both God and money." – Matthew 6:24 There are two distinct camps here - you have to choose one or the other. The separation lines are clear: Master vs slave; love vs hate; devoted vs despised and money vs God. A chasm is clearly visible. It's a case of one or the other, you can't have both things.

Those who seek after money will be consumed by it because it becomes an insatiable force. It controls their body, soul and spirit and propels them in its direction. Enough is never enough. They succumb to this force and love what is evil and hate what is good. What does God require of us? Matthew 22:37-40 says, "Jesus replied: 'Love the Lord your God with all your heart and with all your soul and with all your mind.' This is the first and greatest commandment. And the second is like it: 'Love your neighbor as yourself.' All the Law and the Prophets hang on these two commandments."

Scripture tells us to love the Lord with ALL your heart. This is the first commandment found in Deuteronomy 6:4-5. Why is it number one? It is repeated in Matthew 22:37, Mark 12:30 and Luke 10:27. This repetition is there for a reason; we are to stop and ponder its message and implication. It prevents us from being lured into the pitfall that Satan himself engaged Jesus in before the start of His ministry. Matthew 4:8-10 says, "Again, the devil took him to a very high mountain and showed him all the kingdoms of the world and their splendor. "All this I will give you," he said, "if you will bow down and worship me." Jesus said to him, "Away from me, Satan! For it is written: 'Worship the Lord your God, and serve him only.'"

Loving God does not mean having a life without money and being poor. On the contrary, we lack nothing when we put God at the epicentre of our lives. Psalm 34:10b says, "Those who seek the Lord lack no good thing." Notice, the next command in Matthew doesn't say 'labour and set up your kingdom on earth' (get yourself established financially) but rather 'love your neighbour as yourself'. Why? When you serve God faithfully with all your heart, you have compassion on your fellow man. Those who run after material wealth have blinkers on; they do not see the plight of their suffering fellowman. Not only do such people become a slave to their money, they despise others less fortunate as well. Sadly, when they die, they meet a sorry end and all their wealth cannot save them. The story of the rich man and Lazarus found in Luke 16:19-31 aptly illustrate this point of serving money.

Psalm 112:1 says, "Praise the Lord. Blessed are those who fear the Lord, who find great delight in his commands." There is divine covering over those who make God Lord of their lives. Psalm 112: 6-8 adds, "Surely the righteous will never be shaken; they will be remembered forever. They will have no fear of bad news; their hearts are steadfast, trusting in the Lord. Their hearts are secure, they will have no fear; in the end they will look in triumph on their foes." This means that their devotion to God will be rewarded in time. ◊

When broken is needed

Broken things are often discarded. However, sometimes a thing has to be broken to be used. Gold and diamonds are highly sought out commodities. In their raw state, they are just clumps of dirt. That dirt needs to be broken up to retrieve the hidden treasure within. Even so, there needs to be a refining process for that precious substance to gain its full worth and distinctiveness.

Think of a coconut - it's just course texture on the outside. To get to the useful part; a coconut has to be cracked. You need a hard tool or firm stone to crack that strong, outer shell. Then only can you enjoy the beautiful substance inside.

We too undergo a similar process in order to get the best out of us. It is only in a crisis that we show our true colours; the true grit of what we are made of. We often surprise ourselves during such times. An orange has to be squeezed to get out its nourishing juice.

Within ourselves, there are elements of imperfection that make us flawed human beings. We desire to do the right thing but that doesn't always happen (if we are truly honest with ourselves). Our sin nature gets the better of us. Apostle Paul had that predicament too; he said in Romans 7:20 (NKJV), "Now if I do that which I would not, it is no more I that do it, but sin that dwells in me."

Like the gold, diamond and the coconut, we need to be broken and stripped of the characteristics and old habits that hold us down. When we are 'purified', that's when the true, hidden beauty comes out. So, broken is essential and useful for real, unparalleled beauty of spirit and soul to shine forth. ◊

A Star is born …

Christmas is often associated with that magical time of the year. You sense it in the air – there is excitement and anticipation. Christmas heralds the culmination of the old and the anticipation of the new. Old and new intersect during this time; old is the past – the challenges, the regrets and the memories of days gone by, days that are never coming back. New means the things we look forward to, the changes that follow and the prospects of a brighter future. There is this lingering hope that things will ease up and life will be better, perhaps.

The people of Israel looked to the prophets for words of deliverance and the hope of a Saviour. Isaiah's prophetic utterances were joyfully received but there was a long waiting period. Then it happened as foretold … a star signaled that a child was born through virgin birth. Isaiah 7:14 says, "Therefore the Lord himself will give you a sign. Behold, the virgin shall conceive and bear a son, and shall call his name Immanuel." This is no ordinary event; in fact, it has never happened in the history of mankind. Isaiah 9:6 says, "For unto us a Child is born, Unto us a Son is given; And the government will be upon His shoulder. And His name will be called Wonderful, Counselor, Mighty God, Everlasting Father, Prince of Peace." Note the key attributes: child, Son, government will be upon His shoulder signifies powerful ruler, furthermore His name symbolizes all embracing – Wonderful (Being), Counselor (our guide and therapist, Mighty God – (He is God Himself), Everlasting Father (for ever and ever), Prince of Peace (no more calamity and wars – just peace reigns). Jeremiah 23:5 says, "Behold, the days are coming, declares the LORD, when I will raise up for David a righteous Branch, and he shall reign as king and deal wisely, and shall execute justice and righteousness in the land."

We say famous singers and actors are 'Stars' yet we soon find out how flawed they are. Still, many people slavishly follow these 'stars', spending vast amounts of time, money and resources that make these individuals super stars. All their glitter and glamour evaporate as dust between our toes, when, like a flickering candle our 'stars' are gone. John 3:16 says, "For God so loved the world, that he gave his only Son, that whoever believes in him should not perish but have eternal life." This Star shines ever so brightly and will never cease to exist. Jesus came as a child, a Son like no other and will return as Ruler and King like no other. He will establish His Kingdom in truth and righteousness and His reign will be for eternity. The question is – will you be in His Kingdom? Is Jesus your shining star?

For Christmas, may you too see the reality of the advent of the birth of Jesus Christ, whose sole purpose was to reunite man to God. The next time He comes as Judge and Ruler. John 1:9-14 sums it up perfectly – "The true light, which gives light to everyone, was coming into the world. He was in the world, and the world was made through him, yet the world did not know him. He came to his own, and his own people did not receive him. But to all who did receive him, who believed in his name, he gave the right to become children of God, who were born, not of blood nor of the will of the flesh nor of the will of man, but of God. And the Word became flesh and dwelt among us, and we have seen his glory, glory as of the only Son from the Father, full of grace and truth." You don't want to miss out! ◊

****

Other Works:

Books are available online and in print version. Contact the author via her website for your copy.

1. You Don't Have To Settle For Second Best! A Life Of Hope, Courage And Determination

ISBN – Softcover: 978-1-4931-3410-6

ISBN – E-book: 1493134108

2. Through His Eyes – What We Did To Overcome Depression

ISBN – Softcover: 978-0-9925761-2-7

ISBN – E-book: 978-1-3794730-3-1

3. SOUL FOOD – Renew Your Mind!

ISBN – Softcover: 978-0-9925761-0-3

ISBN – E-book: 9781493134090

4. SOUL FOOD – Restore Your Soul!

ISBN – Softcover: 978-0-9925761-1-0

ISBN – E-book: 9781311074973

5. SOUL FOOD – Look Up!

ISBN – Softcover: 978-0-992576141

ISBN – E-book: 9781370695522

6. SOUL FOOD – Follow Me!

ISBN – Softcover: 978-0-9925761-6-5

ISBN – E-book: 9781005941659

7. SOUL FOOD – There's Hope!

ISBN – Softcover: ISBN: 978-0-9925761-7-2

ISBN – E-book 9780463127223

8. Liberating Others

Written by Shaylan Daniel Ramnath, Edited by Linda Pearl Ramnath

ISBN – Softcover: 978-0-9925761-5-8

ISBN – E-book: 9780463825402

Books co-written by Linda Pearl Ramnath:

9. Stories of Hope – Powerful Testimonies of Encouragement

Linda Pearl Ramnath is one of the co-authors of Authors For Christ:

ISBN – 13: 978-1535076159

ISBN – 10: 1535076151

10. Let Hope Arise: Powerful Testimonies of Hope and Encouragement

Linda Pearl Ramnath is one of the co-authors of Authors For Christ:

ISBN – 13: 978-1540884237

ISBN – 10: 1540884236

Connect with Linda Pearl:

The author is a mental health advocate and blogger here:

http://www.donotsettleforsecondbest.com

Subscribe to my blog:

https://www.donotsettleforsecondbest.com/blog/

Follow me on Twitter:

https://twitter.com/_LindaPearl

Follow me on LinkedIn:

https://www.linkedin.com/in/linda-pearl-ramnath

Favourite me at Smashwords:

https://www.smashwords.com/books/search?que r y=Linda+Pearl+Ramnath+

Thank you for reading my book 'SOUL FOOD – There's Hope!'

This booklet is the fifth of the series of SOUL FOOD. Like all the previous Soul Food booklets, I have put together people's real-life experiences to provide hope and enrichment to you, the reader during these uncertain times. To obtain any these books, go to my website, Amazon or any leading bookseller for your print book or digital version.

http://www.donotsettleforsecondbest.com

****

About the Author:

Linda Pearl Ramnath was born in South Africa and immigrated to Australia with her family. She holds a Master's degree in Education and a Bachelor of Arts in English, Psychology and Biblical Studies. She is a professional writer and editor. As an English and Psychology lecturer, Linda was drawn to books and the workings of the human mind. Her travels around the world expanded her horizons and enriched her understanding of the uniqueness of people. Linda Pearl spent most of her professional career working amongst indigenous groups and marginalized people. She is a devout Christian and is actively involved in community outreach programs. Linda Pearl is a nature lover and enjoys cooking, baking, gardening, creative arts and of course reading and writing. She endorses this quote, "Words are like seeds; we plant them and they produce their own harvest."

****